ANIMALS WITH HUMAN VOICES

ANIMALS WITH HUMAN VOICES

DAMEN O'BRIEN

RECENT
WORK
PRESS

Animals with human voices
Recent Work Press
Canberra, Australia

Copyright © Damen O'Brien, 2021

ISBN: 9780645008951 (paperback)

A catalogue record for this
book is available from the
National Library of Australia

Cover image: Zetong Li via unsplash
Cover design: Recent Work Press
Set by Recent Work Press

recentworkpress.com

SS

for Lisa, Isaac and Aiden
the best poems I ever read

Contents

ANIMALS WITH HUMAN VOICES

MEASURES OF TRUTH

HOW THE ANGELS COVET HEAVEN

THE LINE MARKER'S TESTIMONY

Animals with Human Voices

A Rainbow Made of Soil

If I am lost, I have been lost since I was born.
There are no gods for worms, we are each alone.
How would a god find me, scratching in the dark?
I am lost then, tinkering in the bitter rind of the Earth.
My roof thuds with the shambling footsteps of dumb animals
who follow what they see: clipped stars, the fumbling moon.
That seems too harsh a path. Narrow choices, a terrible light.
I am mostly soil, nudging in the red throat of darkness
and the soil moves through me, making its blind promise,
its digestive ethics. All my paths are innocent.
I have written in the book of the earth and left a bible
that no one shall ever die for. There is no evil
in the Earth, there is no striving, there is only the
warm ruminations of roots and flexing shoulders of fungi.
If I am lost, it is only that I have never needed
to know my destination. When the pounding fingers of rain
tap on the Earth's scalp and the sod soaks to the brimful
and I rise gasping to the spade's scooped surface,
nothing will save me from the flood. If every fleck and
pith of soil I chew on is equal, each end is righteous.

Eyes

The Trilobite's eyes were chipped calcite marvels
that had a million years of ocular dominance
and then vanished in a blink.

Before our plexus of nerves, there were first
lapidary conjunctions of a thousand eyes,
polished and faceted to other spectra.

When the silt of the old oceans
was churned over the last of these lions,
what light was caught in the cold amber earth?

What light was pressed on the lens of each stone
that is forever lost?
The visions and the miracles and the first black wave.

Day of the Spiders

Across the blowing fields of stars
the spiders lay their sheets of silk:
the drying sails of master mariners,
the trampolines, the circus tents,
the spinnakers, the knotted tights,
rippling to the wind's rip, rent in
the wind's trap, flip and flex of
diamond strings, anchors and cast
hooks of spun stuff, stardust,
whiskers and filaments, thready wire
radial and fanning, pleated and snug,
the vibrating coils of nothing, the
strings burning into being, noodling
out of air. There was nothing there
yesterday but the same unmarked
weaves, now tamped with mist.
For one day in hottest summer,
the diligent chemistry of spiders
write out this field of stars, making
indelible axis, uncovering angles,
notating the long grass, plumblines,
laser-lengths, sextant bisections,
making the fields pluck and fret like
a strummed harp, like a fleet
of triremes, tacking into the wind.
Once they're gone, their grey cloth
burs and feathers into fragments,
furs out of form, strips back to field.
What is in a spider that it may link
invisible point to invisible point,
stretch inference over abyss, mark
causalities, connect nothing to nothing?
They plume into the air, journeying
from one universe to the next, casual

with their capacity to highlight the
nodes, the arbitrary constellations,
the maps made from a line strung
from ship to ship, passing strangers.
We'll move along those lines
ourselves one day, connecting star-
burst star to the next, every flower
to every other, every burning sun
and every webby heart to every heart.

Mangrove Canal Road

Slack and listless on the tide's loose string
unloved and unburied vessels fall into the
cavities of themselves, comingling with
the mud and the stinking shift of the water.
The Council doesn't want them and their
owners have abandoned them to dereliction,
but some trick of the law, some mangrove
barrister has said they can't be touched.
Children dare each other over and through
the biscuit brittle planks, a pirate flag tatters
on one mast and the white numbers and letters
splashed over their flaky hulls fade to salt.
Nothing will raise them now from somnolence,
the mangrove is the one-way mouth of a crab pot
and mullet flap gasping on the green banks.
At night, while the mosquitos build
their impenetrable walls and the flying foxes
feud and stumble in the trees like the pub's finest,
the wrecks talk to each other about subclauses,
possible loopholes, last ditch appeals,
but their voices get quieter every evening
and their hearings are constantly deferred, waiting
on further depositions or tied up in each storm's
grim sentence and the slow courts of the ocean.

Lady With an Ermine

after Lady With an Ermine by Leonardo Da Vinci

She can only sit for ten minutes more because
his claws draw scatterings of carnelian
under the silk,
prinked chevrons in the material, slipped weft
and the artist already has his roughs.
The Duke of Milan's mistress
is merely the smooth backdrop to
a study in the muscles of denial.
She's a presented chattel, soft innocence
and symbolism, the displayed
bounty of a powerful man.
Under one delicate hand,
a humming untamed heartbeat.
If you have ever held a wild animal
you would know
its stillness is not acceptance:
all bunched bicep or sheathed bolt,
its every furred consideration
is disavowal.
If you are an artist of renown
and can place in the picture what he sees,
you would start with the girl,
prim in her given clothes, her
coiffed hair, her
owned circlet of desire, framed
captivity within frame, like
successive prisons of oil.
Last, the ermine, brushed
with quick strokes,
leaning from her cupped hands
far from intimacy.
Even trained by a steady hand or eye,
even hung for display in Venetian halls,
the ermine may yet escape.

What Happened to the Oysters

In insoluble suburbs, enclaves of old blood, argos and
arks, dynasties and clans cling to the ridges of silty estuaries,
while the tang of white cadmium, the soft leaded water slips
over their ranches, their estates and plantations capped in green
oceans and swirling blue bays. The virus is in Glamorgan and
Pit Water. Now rumours of Dunalley. Blackman Bay is gone
like the Union dead lying unnumbered in smoke and charcoal
choked snow. Dead reefs and sour beds. On the porches and
battlements and crags of their houses, the seaweed washes
through them and the jellyfish fumble and manoeuvre.
The fish pick at their graves. It was the kingdoms and bloodlines,
the little fiefdoms of purity, the Capulets and Montagues,
the cold wars of pride. There was too much between them.
Too much grey snarling ocean, and not enough trust.
It has happened before: Port Stephen's burghers in dismay;
the Hawkesbury's mass graves. Black catchments rusting.
From the window of the Brisbane to Sydney trains the destruction
is a visible testament: little extinctions swirl in the water.
The fish walk out of the waves. There is no pity in the ocean.

Colony Collapse Disorder

We have no responsibility for the bees.
They were born to their lives, we to ours.
The parasites that kill them, and the disease
is for once, not of our making or our powers.

In the grey forest, these tragedies,
the silent hives and palling fall of flowers,
are not our fault. We may save the trees
with a clear heart, in these final hours.

We may save the fruit, without unease,
or even save the hives before they sour.
Over Auschwitz and Dachau, on the breeze,
the bees flew on their own business, not on ours.

No burning cities, no orphans to appease.
The places that our heavy history scours:
the bees were not responsible for these.
The bees are not obliged to farm the flowers.

The Cold Snap

This is Stanthorpe weather: the clouds
draw a fickle quilt over the horizon but
make no rain. We stand nearly in the fireplace,
which is devouring its ironbark like desperation.
One farm over, the gas guns boom on time,
and the Corellas rise desultorily, circle
and return to the remains of the crop.
The scarecrow's salute has stopped worrying
them and there's nothing else to eat but frost.

This is Stanthorpe weather: so the
rain cuts into me while I carry out
the survivors from the coop's massacre,
limp and bloody, shocked beyond reaching.
We plugged last night's entry holes
but the predator has found them now
and will not stop, these hens are lost.
Blood specks the straw and the guns
shout on cue, shaking the chicken wire.

Out of the wind, the town's women
cradle their lattes in the only café they will
drink in. The owner of the other has a
mad son, the boycotters tell me, a killer
of chickens when he was young and when
that herd of sheep were found with the straight
edges of their throats staring at the sky,
gossip said that he'd have been the one with a
steaming knife stumbling away into the dark.

Everyone knows who the killers are.
A neighbour leans over his fence and tells us
of marsupials we've never heard of. Phascogales.
Google has a glamour shot of them, modelling

cuteness and teeth. When your birds are got at
it's the Phascogales shimmying in. Needlepoint smile.
But, he pauses for the sky to roil and brood above,
the frost will bring them to an urgent hunger.
Everyone's heard of them in town but me.

I never witness what has taken the chickens.
Some nocturnal predator, an opportunist
for easy protein. The weather has turned.
The replacement coop stands half built, dripping.
I learn later that the pariah café was firebombed
one night and has closed its doors. The town keeps
its own sentences and justice. The guns keep firing
and the birds lift more slowly every time, but no one
expects more bodies until the weather shifts again.

Laika Was a Dog

Laika did not see the things an astronaut prizes,
the moon rise, the earth fall, the sun sweep
around her like a juggler's trick, gold, blue
and grey balls, because she did not require
windows, and if she barked, or whined
or whimpered, no one heard her, only
the racing beat of her heart was radioed back
to the indifferent Earth, her slow breaths failing.
We care about that part of us we see in
others. What did the Russian cosmonauts see
in Laika? A mongrel from the street, all
ribs and fear when she was caught, all
fleas and promise, not close enough to pet,
but close enough to commandeer and still a
mammal just like us, blood, bone and pulse.
She proved that we might go to space and live,
or for a little while at least, three days
of bewilderment and fear, as her chamber
heated, as she died. Bewilderment and fear.
We've known those feelings too, so we can tell
what it must have felt for Laika in that
locked room mystery, that physics paradox.
We built our statue for her in old Russia,
after one cold war died, before the next begins,
and that's a memorial of sorts, for a maker
of the future. All the harsh and winking lights
tumbling around the world, and once glinting,
one small tomb fell away from all the other
juggler's balls streaking low on the horizon.
As her shuttle arched over one last time, perhaps
 the mutts of Russia bowed their heads, perhaps all
the dogs of Europe barked. We care for what we know,
for what we understand, for what is close to us. We'd
never do that to a dog again, but we don't need to.

Laika burned up long ago, falling homewards
in that claustrophobic kennel she was kept in,
so she is closer to us now than ever,
close enough to almost see the small comma
of her bones, nose to tail, her blistered paws.
First travellers have the hardest maps to make.

Toad

Toad in the garden, which is the same as
a snake in Eden or a crack in a mirror.
Inexpungable blot of evil but
we must try. The castle must be defended
and each can be the mother of an empire,
a pullulating and teeming pathogenesis
threatening to gush out of the gaping mouth
of nightmare, cover the world, flatten the lettuces.

When we were young enough for casual violence
we'd roam through the plush veil of darkness
just beyond the moth-blow floodlights with
cut down golf-clubs and feeble torches, stumbling
and giggling, night-blind and sugar crazy, until
we'd echo-locate the resolute density of a toad.
Wild invisible arcs and that satisfying thump
of bodies. Changeling stones, staring us down.

There was a black plague creeping southward
and Queensland was lost, untouchable and alien,
the language of genocide, not that we knew it then,
the protection of feral snowy river brumbies
for the nostalgia of a poem was years away.
Dot to dot brown spatter of the enemy
laid out on wet season roads and our challenge
was efficient returns, swerving the 4WD in slime.

Inexhaustible armies of malevolence,
but now I can't decide on measures of
humanity: cold frozen euthanasia over the
gassing eternity of asphyxia. We sling
her kicking and indomitable into her own hell,
the bag crackling in the wheelie bin and for hours
her scissoring legs thump out someone's punishment
until ants climb the lid, not offering rescue.

Apocalypse with Goats

On 04 August 2018, in Boise, Idaho, over 100 goats break loose from a nearby field.

You wake to another creature's trumps of doom,
the street full of the ragged bellies and beards of goats,
waxy horns of goats, nodding goats as silent as the tomb.

You find them steady on the roofs of cars, they kneel or rise,
nudging through the neighbour's slatted fence, your trellis.
They turn to watch you with their calm, inhuman eyes.

With their slotted orange eyes, their tombstone teeth,
they stand there, like dazed congregants exiting a church,
confronted by the burning consequences of belief.

A quiet tide of more than a hundred shaggy goats
lost from their own fields and materialising in your street.
You think of Alfred Hitchcock's Birds, of hungry ghosts.

You look for a sign of blood splashed above your door.
You look for hooves peeking from your boots, a devil's
satyr flanks, but you seem no different than you were before.

The men come, mending gates and fences and with wide arms,
shift stubborn beasts, and so the busy world begins
the day with broken flower pots and muddy cloven charms.

This is not your Armageddon, nor your guilt or shame,
but as they're herded and chivvied away into their trucks,
you know there's been a judgement all the same.

Bezoar

Every day a beetle has its bowl of grass.
Every day a nip of mouse is pursed
up in the articulated ribs of an Eastern Brown.
For each breaking of a Heron's fast: a nail of Perch
headfirst gulleted and gone, slideways,
to bone pellet and chalk splatter.
      After all, who eats and who is eaten
is most of the fundamental law of
God, and rule of man, once the granite words of
Thou Shalt are shaved down to the meat.
      Plodding sauropod with galled glut of stone,
sharp gastrolith to husk a gizzard's nut,
for rhythmic crack beneath feather, behind scales.
Saltlick wallow, supper and repast,
for horse lips, snorting elephant and brick-
headed rhino. Mudpie and dirt sandwich to
tactile toddlers, storing their sensory explosion:
snot tang and caustic sliver of soap cake.
      Once in a non-retrieving hound, a starburst
image of a set of keys. Once in the carcass
of a whale, excavations and blubber landslides
revealed the pitted beaks of monster squids:
dense axes and arrowheads, shot in a
war of glimmerings and nitrogen bubbling depths,
and once when the gush and amniotic mess
of small fish were hooked out of the blanched
wound of a Great White, a flop of arm
waved onto the deck like a flailing eel.
      After all, we are only what we eat,
and what eats us inverts the pyramid of teeth:
staphylococcus circus, smearing in our bloat,
putrefactive fungi, motley and carnivorous,
japing puffballs in our ears and at our nose.
      So you eat and eat, or not at all:

abstinence makes the heart grow fonder and the
stomach smaller and ultimately we are finite
transformations and sharings of constant matter.
    For fifteen years the cat ate the same
grey pebbles of cat food, but through dumb
alchemy, made bones and teeth and splits
of needling nails and presents of fur: squeezed
up anonymous and unclaimed sods of bile.
    My daughter harboured hair nibbled from
her ponytail, slick ink nib or shoe lace length,
cribbed nails and flush knuckle blunted. Such swath
of hair in snips and absent-minded bites.
    All clippings caught and swallowed in
twenty years of stress until it heaved in her
like last summer's bale, black smutted or peated,
until it cemented into a stew of rocks and pain:
Rapunzel climbing down her wind of hair
to never leave, a knotted hank crimped
and bouldered in her gut, far from a prince.
    Each day's dinner chipped from briny flowers,
beaked parrot fish scraping up a beach of sand
in cultivated gardens of coral, flocked in water.
    Then there's The Frozen Man, crammed
in a shallow grave of ice, Ibex bacon,
glassy grains of rice, last meal cooling
into petrification in his stomach, as the arrow
that devoured him hung pitiless in the snowing air.
Stones to weigh him down to death. Each post-
mortem begins as we lived, with stomach contents.

The Immortal Jellyfish

I have pulsed through these blue magellanic clouds
of salt, beyond the improbable past that made me.
I have chimed with the deepest bells, mantled
with my brothers. I am what I always was.

I am older than the manta-ray and megalodon, older
than the weariest history of man. I've taken all the pathless
currents of the sea, involuntary and empty, pushed and pulled
where tide has taken me, drifted out of charts.

The urchin with his spiny arms and mouthless mouth
has taken the same road into these undying straits that I
once took. Snib him down to a rag of meat, he'll grow new arms
with time, but I have not learned my lesson, nor will he.

The highlander fighting through the mists of time,
the pearl beneath the sage's tongue, the getting
and the slow retreat of wisdom. I've floated away from
Gilgamesh's lesson: eternity grants nothing to the living.

I am the philosopher's scintilla of dust pinched into a man.
Unravel me to the four corners of the Earth, scatter me
to the wind, I will grow back no different than before,
each divisible and alone. I am, and all of my parts, am I.

Peel me as bitter grape, chew me as old and indigestible gum,
sift me through the filter of a whale: I am the original
imprint of the sea, the matrix and the wafer for each tongue,
the kernel and the seed of the ocean, its origin and its ending.

Was it ambrosia I took once, golden pear or apple which cursed
me to this incarnation of the water? Memory shreds before
the oceans ever drain. I have forgotten my purpose. I am an
aimless agar agar, hoof of horse: because I cannot die, I do not live.

Measures of Truth

The Prayer of Small Men

To all the avian-headed gods,
the secret councils that rule the world,
The Knights, The Old Men, The Illuminati,
the men who censor all our poems
before they're written: please be gentle.
Leave this poem better than I wrote it.

To all the hidden influencers,
the ogres in their business shirts and ties,
manipulators, shadowy conspirators
siphoning my wealth away, and yours:
leave me enough to buy a coffee
and enough coffee in the world.

To all the brash polluters, stealthy
lawmakers, crimson serpents making news,
impervious servants of the people,
who own my body: make me wish
to be owned. May I be beneath your notice.
May my own interests coincide with yours.

To all those in the know,
be forever knowing, all the clubs and
Ponzi schemes and amnesiac business men,
interest groups, may you retain your memberships.
May the system forever support you.
May I always be able to ignore your iniquity.

May you never stomp on mine.

How Else But The Day

Here, rising first on eyes of shells
and fallen basalt top-knot tuff, now gone
Easter Island men, ranked sentinels,
no wonder that the night runs on,

and sparkling next on the swells and crests,
beneath the quiet albatross and pelican
the swordfish jump, the fire's pressed
on each scale. The wind turns, that flaring fan

over the streamers clearing from the pylons by
the Harbour Bridge, the tumbling spark
of the Earth, handing New Year's day on, the sky
pulled out of drowned fireworks and the dark.

The mortar grinding over the Simpson and Gibson,
then steaming on Japan, grey temples carve
out of an early mist, a brief glisten
on street vendor's carts, slunk shadows starve,

now yawning under the Bodhi Tree:
the first wide 'yes' that joins all, now the plod
of cows down to their fields, each rice paddy
blinks, the line of bamboo hats nod.

Scalloping on the beaches of Mozambique,
hot springboks twitch while the hyenas bark
in the velvet of the long grass, Kilimanjaro's peak
brightens, and the Ivory Coast rises out of the dark.

The approach that draws the radar face
of flowers, that turns the targeting tracks
of leaves, in Brazil, the birds rise at the first trace,
light dimples and splits on each swinging axe.

Beaconing and breaking on Andean peaks,
and rushing down to thin the valley snow,
then over the Pacific, one orange streak
and all is a blue cup, rimmed in glow.

No wonder that the night runs on,
with slow feet and weary gaze:
no race, but still a marathon,
and behind it there, the steady blaze.

Dust

"I will show you fear in a handful of dust." —TS Elliot, *The Waste Land*

1.

Libya stains its neighbours with a blush of uprooted dust,
the bloody sunsets of apocalypse and the wilting dismay of
crops dying. Life and death. Soil can't be made, they proved
that in some lab long ago. There is something indefinable
in the regolith that can't be replicated, some secret magic
powder clobbered loose from dandruffed Tinkerbells.
From space, Libya blanches and dries, and its neighbours
rejoice from rich pickings sifting down to dust their crops.
The mouth of the Amazon far away boils with a brown slab
of Brazil, cut from the banks and slides and alligator rushes
every year, scooped out of the sides of old volcanoes to stir
out to sea with the kelp and the busy sharks. In the year of winter
when Krakatoa blew, the ejecta tuffed and sneezing into sleet
was the shape of death and portents and mortality's reminder.
Now trees grow on its wounded flanks and the monster sleeps.
The world's net, scooping through solar wind has repeatedly snagged
crushed meteors and star stuff, and from them life came once,
so the theory goes. Next time, the smoke palling out of space
may be a bruising spray of meteors and the dust will take us.

2.

In the Archives room, the papers are eared and worn, smeared
with a reader's grip. My marks are there—ultra-violet betrayal
of fingerprints and grime, caking the keyboard, crumbing
on the words, flakes of old outmoded messages, flecks of thought.
We're moving to a 'paperless office', consigning the mullock heap
of carbon into history. The photocopy boys rejoice. The shredder
monkeys lay down their friable reams and wash their hands of whiteout.
Filters suck the tang of pollen and disgruntlement out of the office,
comb esters out of the air, catch our mingled disappointments,
the grey transactions, coups and short term gains of business.
Now fingertips are going on-line, and breadcrumbs are shed,
or syphoned there. But these are new particles, cross-cut
out of a new wind and we old serfs still drop our dying cells,
share our ageless and shabby atoms and rebreathe the austere air.
The next filter upgrade, taking pathogens out of the atmosphere,
insurrection out of our minds, lunchbreaks out of our contracts,
spam out of our inbox, may suck up the grit of us in one hoarse gulp,
one backspace, click, delete and nothing will pass through its matrix.

3.

The dust is billowing redly over the container terminal
as articulated trucks shovel containers into its mouth.
In these backlot suburbs there is always a low animal groaning
of freight trains spreading a weekly crop of coal dust,
a charcoal patina to outdoor tables and to asthma lungs.
Here, the mangroves give way to the shaved and torn pelt of
building sites, burnt stubble, open workings and raw dirt.
There is a coked breath rising from each contribution,
entwining and brewing, coating houses with invisible spores.
We are shaken with the spillage of our lives,
the shed detritus of things: the leaves, the hair, the
snowing smoke and matt of men and cats and dogs.
All these things seem pounded in a heartless mortar:
the glass sky, sharp and ragged as a shark's tooth,
the terracotta and ceramic clot of earthy earth, and
between them nothing but an accumulation of dust;
the worship of dust; or baking, flawed cities of dust;
the civilisations pullulating and sweating out of dust
and returning to it, like poor claymation caricatures.

4.

How do we forgive our odours and exhalations?
The residues and sediments that salt and smear
the backwaters and cul-de-sacs of our veins?
The crystals knapping and sharding in each joint?
In the heavy spongy polyps of our cerebellum,
a suspension of plaque accumulates and
time makes its inevitable dissolves of our body.
we are sanded back to pith, and stain, and dust.
Remember man, the priest recites, *that you are dirt*:
spring saplings loamed and aggregated from the earth
to wear a temporary robe of greenery and life,
fated to be cut back to the stump that lifted us up,
the sawdust spattering the soil. But we need no
reminders: the taste of iron in the sandpaper wind
blowing through the wastelands of our bodies.
Our skin twitches with dead cells sloughing
and the weeping chrism of each pore and hair.
Nothing permanent can be attempted. Nothing in the
long average of infinity can be done to clean the world.

5.

The slow wearing and weathering down of time,
the eagle sharpening its beak on shapeless hills,
all drifts of dust and subtle erosions.
On Titan and on Ganymede, and the barren Moon,
the long reward for steadfast creaking around the Sun
is wasted pits and seeps and frozen seas of dust.
A softening of edges: the gentle breeze has
worn away the haft of the axe, and etched at the blade.
We are granted a vision of the suffocating
end of days, when all things put aside and stored
wear down, and the flatlands creep and swirl.
The afterlife is just as dry and pitiless, we suspect
as some gewgaw left languishing on a shelf
fuzzed with the fine cilia of air falling in a still
room forever. All dull brilliance and musty pearl:
hamster wheels and Hades, thirsty lands that wait
for clouds to build and hammer clay. Purgatory
without remorse. Heaven without redemption.

6.

It's on my mind today: the one last permanent thing,
that survives even after cockroaches and scavengers
get their final come-uppance. Smallest reductions possible.
Ur-particles: the scraps from the philosopher's quest
to carve the universe into smaller bits—kernels and specks
and other ontological leftovers defying classification. Atoms
of doubt. Peppercorns of despair. Grains of uncertainty.
First principles and prime movers. Intangibles and axioms.
However finely powdered, these yield no flash or bang.
What does? Not my works. Cleaning the house today
is an exercise in futility. Entropy is winning.
Each expenditure of energy is a small failure,
the world cools and tomorrow the dirt accretes again.
Nature abhors a vacuum and punishes its accomplishments:
all my rearrangements of the dust, all my wheezy bags.
My unswept floors are cast and sprayed with the same matter
that makes up the blousy fire of the cosmos. No doubt,
nature hates my duster too, and places behind me new grains
to coat each work, as if to say, *all of this too is dust*.

Logical Fallacies of Alien

generalisation
> Ripley's first failure was one
> of generalisation: that one alien's
> elemental viciousness could be ascribed to all.

gambler's fallacy
> that the late acid savagery of
> subsequent samples was similarly brutal
> proved nothing. Repeatedly.

divine fallacy
> the Giger-counter leap at intuition:
> designed brutality, made monstrosities,
> but evolution is its own hidden actor.

two wrongs make a right
> after the Nostromo was scoured
> and the crew had been killed by the alien, in turn
> Ripley punched it into space. Wrong follows wrong.

slippery slope
> but Earth must be saved: fragile teardrop,
> one alien loosed there, like cognitive bias
> becomes the seed of doom. Certainty from assumption.

appeal to emotion
> smudged waif stalked by demon
> and my favourite of the movies. Ripley rasping
> *get away from her, you bitch.* My gut flips.

appeal to motive
>   psychopathic automaton, then self-sacrificing
>   robot helper, androgynous and anodyne companion,
>   homunculus hubris. Each robot different—all suspect.

false analogy
>   sleek futurism and vicious intent,
>   'strong' women battling impossible odds, but
>   Alien is not Terminator, Sigourney not Linda.

appeal to morals
>   in direct proportion to their moral infamy,
>   bit parts snatched into crawl spaces, darkness.
>   Death comes last to crims with golden hearts and innocents.

post hoc ergo propter hoc
>   was it in the misty unfolding of an egg, a cause
>   for all the disasters that ensue, that suffocating hand
>   or hidden machinations, the static SOS disturbing their sleep?

argumentum ad hominem
>   every time, she is Cassandra prophesying
>   but the three-movie deal was so good she made a fourth.
>   sometimes from the mouth of madness, sanity speaks.

Alternative Energy

Absolute finite reservoir of hope.
Total tangle of tap-wires stealing.
The box can't take it, the neighbourhood shorts
and we're busted back to vague expectation.
Fundamental limitations on love.
Speculator bubble, and when the stock crashes,
Anonymous Masks, sour milk and
a rash of government enquiries. Some report.
Definitive volume of truth.
Cisterns and vats and troughs of facts
rising to the displacement watermark
and drifting like an algae scurf.
The float of fake news, all surface and slime.
Measurable pockets of joy.
Reserves and fields and exploitations of barrels
burning the midnight oil with stadiums
of cretaceous legacies, but not a single
new drop to be found anywhere. The cars
roll to a stop on unnecessary roads.
We'd burn all our happiness to keep warm.
When the resource wars, the food queues
empty out the absolute extent of joy,
what will we have? A brief fire. Empty wells.

A Survey of Australia's Religions

Thirty per cent of Australians indicated they had no religion
—Australian Bureau of Statistics

        but we have saints taking Selfies, photo-shopping in halos,
or proselytising on the blogosphere, defending moral positions
with Emojis, their articles of faith with unfriending, texting psalms
and chants and hymns of praise, diet tips and cat photos;

        and there is worship in the reeling of a barramundi.
Sun God and sacrifice, brandished and measured
and every Sunday, burnt offerings send their smoke to heaven
from Webbers and from Bunning's best bargains;

        the ecstatic possession of holy fools rolling their eyes
outside a Saturday-night RSL, punch drunk and brawling,
king hits and confessions, pouring bitter into gutters,
sloshing sneakers and the scuffed floors of paddy wagons;

        you have your churches, Australia:
bright cathedrals roaring at each goal, heads bowed
in solemn hope of miracles, 20 points down, five minutes
to go, down by the Yarra, rained on at the Gabba;

        all the sacraments most precious, dispensed at
ten to eight and half past nine, at the Human Bean, the
Black Market, the Steam Room and the Mug,
transmuting manna at $5 a cup, 50 cents for soy;

        the Houses in their rites and disputation,
introducing defamation under Parliamentary Privilege to
the greater glory of God, ecumenical or schismatic in Bennelong,
tearing down false idols in bellwethers;

we are not bereft of devotion, we are
downloading the thousand names of God via Google Film,
giving praise to Netflix, taking in vain House of Cards,
counting blasphemies through the seasons of Game of Thrones;

the hollow stations of our pity:
third in OECD averages for charity at home, blowing out
for disasters and plagues overseas, our angels walk the same
streets as angels everywhere, asking *are you all right?*

abandoning the pews for sticky bus-stops,
pressed wet-grass parks, backbone and heel prints on damp dunes.
Oh the observances on all the edges of this land! Plunging
into the mystery of the waves, each day riding the ineffable into the beach;

come wash your souls, come be shriven, where men
can beat their wives in the inviolable altars of their bedrooms, and
for zealots with gang tattoos and motorbikes, in the overflowing barbwire
Eden of Goulburn, no sinner cast out, no penitent forgiven;

the broken providence of the desert, the defiled chapels
of the bush, we pay our respects to elders past and present,
chroming on the fast track to God under each overpass, generations
of despair, paying credit on their crosses with welfare cards;

I am too full of God for the Productivity Commission,
too empty for the Unions, I have tithed to the ATO
and given freely to the Day Care Centres, I have stood
with the faithful in the queue, I have given unto Caesar what is Caesar's;

revile the heathens for they produce
no takeaway cuisine to brighten our polity, for they have
tried to enter heaven by boat, let the heretics
be sent to Manus, or exchanged for fanatics out of Bankstown;

cant and spirituality, madrassas and yeshivas
for all: the Telegraph, the Herald, the Financial Review intone
victimhood, elitism, left, right, do-gooders and political correctness,
nothing can be said, everything is permitted;

Jedi believers in the Force are up, extolling
the virtues of light sabres in chat rooms, Wiccans down,
but the Messiah from Bowral has not yet returned and we
wait, staring at dead reefs and cleared forests for the end of days;

there is much faith here, brother, but little belief:
the coal fired bishops, the steel refining cardinals, cattle popes.
We have much to be thankful for, much to praise:
a God for every voter, a ceremony for every day.

Measures of Truth

1. The Cold Hard Truth

We have been pulling hairs of ice out of
Antarctica's thousand-year frozen pelt
for the sake of the world's contested forensics.
Pulling out a white frost thorn, milky,
compact, and hard as an age of poison.

The Romans, warming their fingers at
the great forges of Tuscany and Brittany
while a vicious winter hissed on the coals
and dusted them with snow, are found in
a haze of iron, rusting the core of ice.

Nothing is ever hidden from the Earth, it
is incised, intaglio'd in some far corner,
pressed like old music in the tar of memory,
ashed like fingerprints, and folded away for
a rainy day, a century of rainy days and floods.

Disgruntled wives dosing their husbands' dinners.
Russian spies ticking and sallow with polonium.
It's all in the chemistries caught in a hair. No one
gets away with murder. Spun in misty centrifuges
we pull out cold witnesses from the core of snow.

The truth is always hardest to believe, though
the black coke marbles each spear of blue ice,
though the sea salts a rime to the top paddock, and
the virgin ice-cores stained with 400 years of smog,
sleep in university labs, cowled like a morgue.

2.   *The Statute of Limitations*

To be honest, he blurted it out too late. He told
the birds, who told the wind who told the trees
but none of them could act, or care, and so the world
did not know to end, or his wife to leave him or
his children abandon him, for his gust of secrets.

To be honest, the statute of limitations had
always applied and his fear of getting old and
losing the careful grip on his tongue, or that the
lock on his throat would dissolve with dementia,
reached the sunset clause. Loose lips sink ships.

To be honest, all the dams burst in his head
and he muttered to the stars and he shouted at the
bedpan and he mumbled to his nurses and he gushed
and spilled with knowledge. So they raised his medication.
There was no one left to know his truth from fiction.

To be honest, he'd held the lie so long against disclosure,
his words a cyanide pill, a loved and hated truth, that
he alone could understand its value, could speak of history
like it was fresh, like the dust had not covered it long ago,
like the wound had not melted back into his skin.

To be honest, why he ever kept his secret, like
a locket or a keepsake, was lost with all his memories,
all the reasons and any chance for forgiveness.
Like the cruelty of old Greek gods, age took away
his many truths and gave him back his one lived lie.

3. *Drunk Spiders*

Getting a spider drunk like it's on a date, dropping
a tablet fizzing to the bottom of its drink, or offering
it something harder—it's the spider's first time on cocaine
and it needs a safe place to come down. Brewing it
up a black, worried that you have ruined it for art.

But it knits and spools things in its dervish:
disjointed shard-webs; obsessive geometries, slow
spiritual spirals which trail into nothing, and
it could not have done those sober. It needs the
chemical muse, to make art no spider can make.

Juiced up flies, and suddenly the spider can do
anything, take on anything, net the world's bug,
gantry and scaffold the coruscating stars. Correlation
and deviation are at the heart of science and
the news is in: every spider creates the same drunken art.

The probative value in dealing drugs to a spider,
being an arachnid's enabler, is finite. The spider
in a man's head makes wild tears of webs and
poor art. How much of any intoxicating work is spun
from the heart, how much is slipped into our drinks?

Coleridge, Baudelaire and Burroughs, emptying
their heady vein of words, made skeins and patterns
of their lines, but how much was the drug, how much
genius? The distance between each arc and spoke is
a function of the dose. Anything can be measured.

4. *The Truth Will Make You Free*

A planet is the only test-tube that we possess,
large enough and wide enough and old enough
to encompass the truth. An epochal survey, the
sample size broad enough to be conclusive.
All the rest is randomness and bloody afterbirth.

We will know when we know, when the silt lies
down long enough to make a fossil. That
will be sufficient time to sweep away all the
Fake News. But the results are not yet in and initial
outcomes could be errors, fluctuations in the data.

When we were still many years from the results,
we put our women out of sight: our daughters
and our wives, too full of grief, too headstrong,
too open with their thoughts, too poor to pay,
imprisoned for their lives in the experiment of doubt.

Down at the Planck Length, everything is grey,
momentary and provisional, universes form and
reform like bubbles on a beach, all of it explainable
away, the observer pulling the tablecloth out from under
the observed, the magician keeping doves inside his coat.

That is why we took our wayward daughters and
our sharp-tongued wives from their homes, placed them
in asylums, named them mad. It took so long to realise
we were wrong. We did not have sufficient evidence.
We needed facts as long as life, as large, as sure as time.

5. Bone Music

It will keep surprising you, this universe, its infinite
humour: storms striating the edges of the galaxy,
and at the still centre, a supermassive black hole
sleeping with a full belly, crumbs on its sleeves,
the burning field of stars laid out like a tablecloth.

Khrushchev walled rock and roll out of Russia,
the radios tattooed Tchaikovsky into listeners eardrums
and records were melted into roads. Prokofiev and
Shostakovich were prescribed by the Soviets and
played to the packed concert halls of the damned.

But the banned music of the West was a Strange Attractor
so Russians scrambled through the backdoor bins
of clinics and hospitals searching for x-ray waste
to etch a record over the ghost of a mandible.
Hip negative ilium. They called it Bone Music.

People will die for the notes of 12 Bar Blues,
for the same reason that people will kill for it,
because it exerts a gravity of its own. When a girl band
protests in a church, or Tibetan musicians are beaten
in prison, something like echoes of drums ripples out.

Nothing is ever truly hidden, not even the silent
refuge of a supermassive black hole, found by sensors
spraying out an x-ray signal across the ordered
marches and triumphal patriotism of space. A little
pulse of sound, not unlike the music in each bone.

The Cole Porter Effect

A piano duel that never happened
between 1900 and Jelly Roll Morton
set alight a cigar on red hot piano wire
incandescent with the passion of their playing
and so the duel was won and jazz was
shown to harbour a fundamental energy, just as
hot as the plasma cooking in an atom.
But the physics doesn't work, and there
are a dozen mathematics majors and
science buffs who wish to explain why
on the pedantry wilderness of the internet,
who point out that the resonant properties of
piano wire change under extreme temperatures,
that the spruce and maple in a Steinway grand
would flash into an ignus crescendo long before.
Other duels that never happened include
Louis Armstrong battling with a djinn,
BB crossing Stratocasters with Charlie Christian
and Robert Johnson bartering his soul
down at some lonely Mississippi crossroads.
Whatever drug is encoded in the swing
beat of the slow tresillo, rough syncopation
telegraph and rag-time blue-toothed into
amygdala centres, there are more than enough
myths packed into the inferno between each note
to set any keys on fire, or a momentary suspension
of the laws of physics. While the music plays,
Lucille can howl and until the music stops and
the final solo finds its way back to the melody,
any legend could tell you that anything goes.

The Wrappings

We eat the sea for Christmas,
honeyed and smeared with
the sea's essence on our fingers,
a scoop of the sea,
fresh squeal of seagulls
on our tongue, sweet muhst
of seaweed in our mouths,
full with the rough of waves.
We eat Christmas with every bite,
all boardshort grit and
the wealthy redolence of
king prawns. Ripe stain
in every shell, myrrh
and frankincense brewed
in each king prawn. For days
we smell the sea on our fingers.
We double bag Christmas,
leave it in the bins near the beach.

Christmas Dinner

The end of year approaching, we return to our places
of birth, like census takers, burdened with expectation.
During the day, the ants make a mad chiaroscuro out of
the invisible heat, whirling their new wings like an after image
of a sparkler, and at night, once the Christmas lights are
switched off, a dull occasional glow of fireflies appears like
the feeble snap of chemical torches. Moth drifts and
stingless wasps pushing against the screen door,
bearding the print of Santa Claus, giving their lives for
a pointillism of smudges peppering the glass.
In the garden's digestive warmth, the inexhaustible
beetles crimp and pinch the leaves and buzz like the high gears
on a clockwork soldier, waving the black struts of their legs.
We force our way down to the beach, through the crush
of the aural battery of cicadas droning at the oscillation
of neon lights and camping fridge motors which clink
the glass of their frozen beers in an endless celebration
of drunkenness, while in the native bee nest, an early gift
for summer, the ladies hunker down and dream of Veroa.
This Christmas holiday is given over to the machinations of
insects: flies leoparding the wheelie bin's ripe promise, persistent
and intimate drinkers at eye and mouth, champagne suicides.
Not a second coming of that shambling beast, but the
excess of some old God, hungry like a curse of locusts,
the pagan pieces of a torn up idol, the legion and
gestalt body of a cumulative deity, winged, carapaced,
antennaed in its manifold creeping and skittering, copious
and crowded, tasting the dry turkey, the curling slivers of duck,
the slumping tomato and wilting lettuce clinging to the beetroot,
the pavlova collapsing and craterous, the fudge, perspiring
and sugary. A new manger, numerous and multiple, pincered
and palping: the chrysalid, pupae'd, maggot spill of Christmas.

How the Angels Covet Heaven

The Careless Shore

That terrible indifference
which expends itself
on cold sand, on the
caked calves of lifesavers,
that boils its energies in
churning the sand,
removing the marks of
footprints, maple leaf
seagull prints
terminating into air,
a child's question marks
flung into the water,
the following constellation
of a dog's claws.
So like the careless
shifting in the dark gut
of the universe which
takes a smut snowball
of rock and ice and
flings it at the Earth:
that brutal disregard
of consequence.
The lifesaver works
for the hours of minutes
at breath and pause
while a silent crowd gathers
and the waves pound
their apathy and erase
the boy from the beach.
Long after the world ends
like a rock hurled
out of an empty sky,
the waves are still rewriting
the pristine sand.

How the Angels Covet Heaven

Perhaps we were birds once, in another life,
careless with the effervescence of the air,
perhaps a pinion or a plume still crowds our
heavy shoulder blades, itching to erupt.
The wake is beautiful at night, quilted as a
featherbed of white, tumultuous and broad and
the cruise ship carries laughter on the breeze, a
string of fairy lights twinkling on each deck,
and if there is sadness anywhere, it gathers here,
fascinated by the things it cannot have, the
weight of love, the heavy burdens of desire.
When a cruise ship leaves its port it carries coffins,
for the passengers who choose to step into
the glorious argument of water, which is the wake,
and discard that part that could not be a bird.

The Beach Eats Boys

Rinds of iron.
Rough crusts of rust.
Sharp arcs and spurls.
Shark-toothed spines
and noduled quartz
break bones,
suck at surfers.
Lathed sandstone
lipped and strewn
in ruined, mars-scapes,
scraped spurs, surf breaks,
fish fissures, weed loaves,
slicked grind groves
and grooves
that slice waves,
rip ribbons and claw coral.
Hard headland shards
takes two children through
green-slipped guts
on Christmas Day.
They grind with the cold crabs,
stirred nibbles of pebbles,
tongued bones of stones
and found shells shored.
The beach breaks boys.

Dinners With Dead People

Jesus
Most invitations go unanswered.
Everyone has him on their guest list.
There is always enough food, if you like fish.
One wine glass only, and the toast is macabre.
No one understands him, he speaks in Aramaic.
He is omnipresent and sits at every seat.
There is an awkward silence at the end.

Einstein
All night you waited for something profound
but all he could talk about was how each course
really hung together and that there was a common ingredient
but he kept changing his mind on what it was.
Not dressed for dinner: dishevelled,
shoes without socks.
He smoked through dessert out on the porch:
the light there was better.

Elvis Presley
Confirming that he is eligible under the criteria,
he denies the aliens and the Mafia theory
with a big wink.
Not at all embarrassed about dying on the toilet,
we learn that real gold toilet seats
are cold and that you can have
bacon, peanut butter, banana and honey sandwiches for dinner.
He sings Hound Dog at the end of the meal.
Blamed Pepsi for the rough notes.

Freud
Witty, erudite and up-to-date on
politics. Trump fascinates him.
You spend the evening avoiding anything controversial
until your husband starts making bad jokes
and punning on Gemeinschaft.
He is a long time in the toilet
but comes out wittier and wiping his nose.
After he leaves, you wonder for ages
what he thought of you.

Your Parents
They are quieter than they used to be
and won't talk about what happens next.
The hug is cursory and they toy with the salad.
You reopen old arguments and
start watching the time.
Your father is shorter than you remember.
Your mother is taller.
You hope they'll comment about the meal:
it's your mother's recipe.
They leave too early.

Cortege for Richard the Third

Rare for a reputation to survive
exhumation from a carpark's foundations,

nor the curve of your deformity,
but they set the record straight

on that, and on your paternity. It seems
that courtly love occasionally was caught,

and that there was much common water rinsed
through the blood of the Regal line,

but not enough to threaten a Prince's sleep.
Time is ample provenance to promote any piece

and there's no set protocol for
reburying a disreputable king.

Your contemporaries had their heads
hefted by their wives in bags, for years,

or sable and ermine torn to four points
and paraded to a pauper's grave.

This fourth act is stranger than the other three,
but the hump, the twins—these are hard to shake.

Richard, you may rest uneasy in Leicester now
with all the pretenders and tabloid kings

but you would not have enjoyed anonymity,
and villains get the loudest ovations.

Atlas Carried the World

Stanislav's hair is burning, like a holy fool crisping
on the pyre of his martyrdom, or berserker, snarling
as he dives among the spears, but Stanislav is silent
as he works, an automaton busy in its code, repeating
the piston hammering of steel. If this were a comedy,
Stanislav would not pause after laying down
the coughing, smoking children, but would return
for greater feats of absurdity, for a chest of drawers,
a bookcase, a baby grand, its ivories lively with a tune,
to collapse a moment on the ashy grass, until at last
he'd go back in and retrieve the fire. If this were
a story, Stanislav would be among the ranks
of soldiers that the mad king sent into the burning
castle, to put out the fire with their bodies
and their blood. But this is not a story, and
after the two children, Stanislav went back in and
did not come out. The fire was too intense, and
this was a two miracle deal, two-for-one. If this was
a movie, the beams would collapse, the fire would
crawl up the walls and the windows blow.
The last camera shot as the whole thing soufflé'd
down, would be of Stanislav, backlit by the glow,
though all the watchers gave him up for dead and
embers mothed his clothes. But he did not come out,
nor were there cameras in 18th Century Bialystok,
so it did not happen, or at least it happened in the
ordinary way these things have always been happening:
a passing stranger sees a house on fire and saves two
sleeping children. He is not refined by flames, nor
become purified. He does not stride out with T-1000's
quicksilver steps, to batter Arnie. He simply bundles
out the children and goes back for their mother. But if you
look carefully, you can see Stanislav carried hundreds out
that day: a doctor, nurses, housewives, even a poet. My

mother and grandmother, her father and her uncle, on those
broad, gasping shoulders. My cousins and me. Armies of
people spreading across the world. How do you thank
the men who run into a fire? You write of Stanislav
who rescued the future from the burning past.

New Born

Full moon patched up over the city's brow:
a last melting scoop of icecream, and under it
years, lifetimes, orbits of water,
turn through the river like fatalism.
If it wasn't for the peek-a-boo clouds
shifting their fickle hands, or the neon
strokes of the moon's barrage, stabbing
its zipper reflection in an elongated chain
over the wave's traffic and desperate mysteries,
then the water would have been a
black void in the night's cold teeth,
and that moment when the river pauses
at the peak of its tide with the outstretched
stations of an initiate limbering through its
meditation, and the fish fumble in sudden
uncertainty, and the ripples mill and freeze
in an unknown ideogram,
before turning back the way they came,
would be unheeded in the night's deepening.
These are the old rehearsals of
career actors washed out of jubilation,
the dog-eared script of the muddy
river, turning its pages, and the grinding
arc of a new moon rolling through the same
carved channels inured to exultation.
Beauty is alloyed into shuttered moonlight
and hammered into the bed of a river
but joy is poured into new things,
minted and coined in new things, like the finite
treasures of a miser's mansion, and on
this moment when we saw the lull in the river
and the plated silver of the moon's melt mirror,
we heard the first passage of a newborn's cry
as it came into the world from

the other night, roaring with the voice of lions,
the stark pain of life, and terrible triumph
of a newborn breathing the ancient ennui of air
and making of it something redolent and momentous:
the necklace of water, the ring of silver,
the original moon pinned above the only river,
and everything made new, new and joyous.

Korora Beach, Dusk

What did I see or thought I saw
as the slatted sun closed down the beach
and the crescent-sanded shadows reached
and fishermen pulled their hooks from the wave's jaw?
I saw a man step helplessly off the break,
or perhaps an Oyster Catcher sewing fish.
I wonder if my breath was a windy wish
held gulped and filtered by Flathead and Flake.

What did I see, or hope I saw?
I saw a man step silently into the panes
of glass and steel, but who knows if he rose again.
Soon I'll pick through the lantana's claw,
but marking the site of a Cormorant's plunge, I stare
at the grey water, until the wind takes a blink.
He's swimming somewhere out there still, I think,
with the strange strokes of a seal, coming up for air.

Ouroboros

The eye that dilates the eye that watches the eye that dilates
the tick that tunes the pulse that tempos the tick of the pulse
the waves that make the waves that turn the waves back into ripples
the feedback in the echo of the echo of the feedback
is reflection on reflection is redirection and inflection
the consequences began long ago, and the centre keeps expanding
the program has a while to run, but all commands have been enacted
now the wings that flap the wings that flap the wings that turn the flock
and the scales that slip past scales that fin the school
are repeating are repeating all the thunder of that beauty
all the widening of pupils and the lips that lip that lick the lips
now God is just the pressing of the pressing on the button
and the rest is ripples scattering and gathering together
o love o love I'm nothing but the feedback in the echo.

Bookend to a Flood

Sky empty of clouds and we chew stubble for weeks
until he tells me we are leaving, but there is nowhere,
the Earth is evaporating into dust and desperation.

The drought reveals the land's knapped skull,
skinned to a grin of granite teeth, the end
of the Earth begins with dust and dubious gifts:

hulls on their blocks, beached beyond any ocean,
piers over dunes far from their tepid shores, the
acid retreat of water, the last days of petrification,

and things better hidden, rummaged into corners,
or drowned for forgetting: dented barrels, wrecks and
disasters, surreptitious concealments, sunken treasure.

The day before we abandoned hope, tossing it like a
wriggling bag of kittens, the scouring dried the middle
of the dam and we could see a bleached and bloated suitcase.

Nothing given over to the nip of eels and poke of turtles
blankly nudging, can do a man good, can re-pour the water
or populate the ossification of our town, dead of thirst,

but my husband dragged it to the cracked margins of the dam
grunting about salvage and stood staring at it with
the raw eyes of a fortune teller whose card will not turn.

I thought of Pandora cupping shadows and a curse, I
thought of the emptiness to be found in a Magician's hat, I
thought of the bundles buried underneath a silent threshold.

He broke the old locks and swore at the contents, stumbling from the bones of a little girl sleeping, here in the water of the district's last dam. Now there's truly nothing to hold us.

I wonder how long she huddled there drowning, while the great drought baked us, and how long in turn will the wind push us to wander. Until rain falls again to cover all our secrets.

Rules for the Dead

The dead are thin as baking paper.
They jostle each other on numb feet.
They have long ago given up waving at the living.
They may have been turned from the gates by silent angels.
They may have knocked with cold fists, without answer.
There is no space in the crowded earth
that does not throng with weak shadows and sad spirits.
The dead may not touch the living.
The dead must watch chewing and teeth cleaning.
They shall listen to snoring.
They may not change the channel when it is on home purchasing.
They are jaded with sex and aghast at love.
The dead have seen every showing of the Sound of Music.
The dead know how it all turns out.
The dead may not change.
The dead may not turn away.
The dead have no mouths, but they may keep their eyes.
They have no eyelids.
They do not sleep.
There are more of the dead every day, pushing
and stumbling from wherever the dead are made.
The dead may be safely ignored
but the living should be watched carefully.

The Line Marker's Testimony

Fruit Picking

Seamus is four trees further up the row
under a blousy broad-brimmed hat he's found
in some junk store, and painter's smock, I go
more slowly, and cover the same ground.

The yellow-tailed black cockatoos shrill
at the laden edges of our day's claim.
By the grey ends of sunset, both our buckets fill
to the same level, and our wages are the same.

I let Seamus barter with the women
who own these fields. There's something about
an Irish brogue. I bend the ears of the men
to ask for work, and often go without.

Each fruit has its way, its caprice,
but blueberries have always been my friend.
When they are ready, the stems release
so simply into my cupping hand.

There's always more on each branch, they ripen
in stages, as if to give each bird its chance
and every dusty fruit-picker his season.
We pluck together in an easy trance.

Up and down each row, under an aching sun,
I follow behind to make sure each tree's complete.
He clears out the larger and closer ones,
but I always find the smaller fruit as sweet.

The Line Marker's Testimony

I like to pick up hitchhikers, though there are less
each year who'll dare to stick their thumb out
since Ivan worked up and down these roads and since
his avatar terrorised Wolf Creek for television,
but young tourists still have a go, pack-muling
their bright-eyed way across the country.
I didn't make it all the way through high-school
but I still remember my teacher drew a line on the
board and said if I could sight along its edge
I'd never see it turn, its spearing point
the only thing that ever approaches eternity.
I've had kids who were stretching their gap-year over
a season picking fruit, thumb down my ute, speak
to me about the pools around the stars, the sleepy, heavy-
lidded stars, and the deepest dark where nothing
can escape, not even straight-lines diving into sleep,
so I know there's more to geometry than that.
I curate the longest graveyard in the world,
set the catseyes, place the speed signs, clear the
weedy edges, but most of all, I paint the centre line,
help it seam the mountain's coil and edge,
camber, drift and slipway, zip and unspool,
the thread that leads out of the ranges again.
Sure, I've seen those photos shared around the Net:
paint rolled right over carrion, random gaps,
zigs where the road zagged, as if the workmen
were asleep at the wheel, or oblivious and blind,
but that is not my way. I maintain the busy corridors
of the living through the black-spots of the dead,
and when I come upon the many crosses that make up
the turns, and dips and cutaways of my road,
I do my best for every cairn, clear away the weeds, set
the wreaths of plastic flowers back upright.
I've seen it all: the trucks looming out of darkness

the cloudy Milky Way dipping into eucalypts, slow
cyclists pumping pneumatically up the hills,
stubborn koalas sitting with their backs against the edge,
kangaroos staring down a driver's headlights, and
I know the truth of white lines in the dark, how easy
it is to sink into gravities of doubt, how a vehicle might
drift from its purpose, how a driver might wander off
the road, slip yawning into gullies and be lost. So
I like to pick up hitchhikers now and then, pale
in the uncertain wash of the high-beams. Perhaps
I'm taking some of the dead further on, exorcising
this quiet mausoleum, straightening out the curvature
of space, helping ghosts make their disoriented way home.
I paint the road that takes the straight path out of time.

The Eighth Strike

These seven times, and now I am a footnote and a search result. I am
'verified' by Guinness, and rashed with a vine of branching exit scars.

My wife has become distant: she shifts from me to the edge of propriety.
Our bed is broad. On a clear day I was found by a strike that stung between us.

I miss the company of others, but who would be friendly with a bomb? Only
those who make their homes on a fault line with the careless spirt of gamblers.

If I was tuned for this, like a pure quench of metal, each pinning blow
would not be so hard, but I am a trickle of iron filings slowly lining up.

Outliers allow an average. But in the scale of plasma, there must be some other man
whose life is shot with the negative of my strikes. What would such a life look like?

I feel struck by a deliberate malice: sought out by an abandoned tarantula of a god,
dissipating its petty godhead in vengeful thunderbolts or karmic Russian roulette.

But I am no villain or demon, and my ill acts and wasteful omissions are no worse
than any other man, less than some. There is no justice in each electron scourge.

Perhaps on the inside, where only lightning looks, I am taller than other men,
perhaps I am a clearer conductor. I console myself with thoughts like these.

My EEG is regular, my CT scan unprepossessing. It is not enough. I refuse to
bury myself with randomness, some lotto winner, some un-earned freak show.

The moment of each bolt is visitation: seizure-white like the mistranslated ecstasy
of the possessed; loudhailer message from God; voice of angels, never understood,

and then only ash, burn and sear, secondary fire and filler news story.
These are not amorous kisses and lightning does not know how to love.

There may never be another strike, and I refuse to fear the sky, or the storm's leafy fury.
If another bolt waits for me wound like a spring, I will be ready. This time, I will be ready

The Handshake

When he reached out his hand to you,
the father of the boy your government had
murdered for a policy, or so the papers said,
you did not take it. Why was that?
Perhaps you felt he offered something heavy
as a neutron star, slick in-falling burden
of despair, too hard to grasp, or gift
of unwanted knowledge, poison chalice of
truth, the wither and the charring of that
inconvenient light, which torches out self-
deception. Perhaps you know that you can
stopper up your ears, can hold your heart
in the cold ocean between each beat, can
place a lock upon your tongue, if you must,
but a handshake is part of the oldest language
and will disclose what you hold back, what
the politburo, apparatchik wish you not to say,
rehearse it though you might: limp fish, sweaty
or dry palm, masterful and firm, crush
and domineering, pull-in and shoulder squeeze,
tool of politicians and of stars, but
more is taken in a handshake, then is given,
comfort if it is offered, or disdain, the
reaching out of two creatures separated by
a frangible and uncertain strait, the cellular
barriers of policy and position, and grief,
which is the yawning chasm over all. Perhaps
none of this: you'd turned away, the cameras
flash and fruitless dissections fill tomorrow's news.
So few opportunities to reach out, so few to take,
to show amity and kindness, in our separate
galaxies of skin. Perhaps it was a media
stunt, an impossible trap, an ambush of
ideologies, but you cannot hide from

a handshake, and to shake a hand both men
must come close enough to touch and wear
each other's fingerprints burning on their skin.

The Superman Complex

He cannot stop the bullet
which kills him. He cannot
fly. Balconies attract him:

the drunk desire to lean out
and test the ropes of air.
The wind presses

and releases him. The party
is tired, and Superman bores
him. Just another alter-ego.

He has aged into the myopia
of Clarke Kent's glasses, the
lycra is tight around his waist.

When he was making
thirteen episodes a year
the suit fitted, the cape swirled

and he could have reached out
to the cars as he crossed the street
and stopped them with his palm.

Johnny Weissmuller drowned in fame.
Adam West fled the bat's shadow.
George was once the Man of Steel.

No other role could suit him
and he gave up trying. The party
bores him: middle-aged lovers.

The power has left him. He wonders
if the villains are laughing somewhere:
sirens wailing in storyboard prisons.

Despite his days of kryptonite,
he fancies in the final scene that
he could catch the bullet in its flight.

The Nave

Eighty-six kilometres past the last
trickle and rust service station, a weatherboard
church stands listlessly at the roadside, like
a broken-down hitch-hiker; one of those
mad chapels which rise out occasionally from
the junk bush, as if they were shaggy prophets
striking out into the wilderness; one of those
inns of last hope, built by the community
to make a community, and knuckling on
when the community fades into failed farms.
Every window was broken. Every window.
One hundred years combined of stained glass
wages, and small denominations collections.
Probably stones. Someone must have really
hated this rickety old church, and come equipped,
as the police might say, with malice,
systematically putting out God's eye, halfway
between anywhere important and somewhere else,
a trudge by foot and three albums by car.
There is such an urge to break things, to
set a hand against the plinth of the Earth,
and push it over, such an urge, to make
unseen corrections to the stolid dependability
of creation. Some say that a devil is in it,
whispering in our ears, or grain by grain
encouraging the avalanche, but I keep thinking
of that story you told me of your weary
colleague who chips at the edge of parenthood
with a terrible love, nursing three years
of unresponsive childhood from her daughter,
pulling a rope of gasping nights slowly
over her shoulder, reeling in the future.
Sometimes God gives us something broken:
little towns, worshipping their stubborn way

through drought and flood; or little lives,
silent and unblinking in their cots. Like all fatuous
truths, we are told things which are broken
allow us to see such beauty limned and split
from the hale world, like a flash of colour
struck prismatic from the stain of a bloody
crown of thorns; or this rendering of Peter
rent by a vengeful rock pitched through a pane;
half broken apostles range and glint in the apse.
But each unremittent stone in the jagged brow
of the church doesn't seem to have brightened this
dusty cul-de-sac of nothing on the way from nowhere.
Poor testament to faith and industry. God should do
better with his lesson. I choose a stone, take a throw.

The Map-Maker's Tale

She came in through the clatter of the doorway,
behind her the squalling storm like a wave's black tongue

and in her hands a sheaf of maps and mildew
and franked and mothy deeds to lands

long washed out of the way by indifference and
the blue melt and the green gloss of the ice.

I had to tell her that I had no jurisdiction
below the greedy fingers of the highest tide,

that her father's promises and titles had been drowned
when the islands had gone under and the shores

had climbed up the First World's sneer to the hills.
The old lives that we followed have been overturned,

the lines we stood behind with our shields and swords
and told the world it could not take its shelter,

all overrun, all gone into a swallow and the world's
poor wander whether we will it or not.

She cursed me as a whale might curse a hunter,
as a spear might curse the hand that flung it,

and took back those deeds, the wax and paper
which proved to be a poor seal to the water, to the

welling and washing of her ancestors, the salting of
her ancestors in their lost graves. She warned that

she went to treat with one who owns the water,
that on nights like this I should sit uneasy in my office

where all the lines of yes and no are tangled
and blur and twitch like so much compromise,

for the storm is blowing straight against my door
and it blows the tide behind it to heights before unknown.

She turned and left, her hair wild as the weather, and
where she'd stood, the brief puddle of her leaving

formed a map I have little power to decipher and none
to alter, and by the door, a single sequin scale.

No End of Endings

We've had at least five saviours knocking on our door.
'Show us your wounds!', we shout. They form a little line.
Angels with burning swords, a baker's dozen, more.
Demons raging in the darkness, until Sarah changed the sign,
it reads 'no hawkers and no messengers from God', but there's no end
of endings, or the apparitions that they send.

Rain of fire. Meteor strikes. What can heaven send
we haven't seen before? We leave saucers of milk outside the door
for the elves, but they're not taking them anymore. The end
of days is taking longer than it should. I've seen a line
of suns cross the horizon, a cracked moon, other signs.
But Sarah calls it hedging my bets, as if I needed one sign more.

What kind of numbers are required for a horde? More
than a dozen zombie neighbours I'm guessing. We can't send
any messages or look up any definitions. There's no sign
that Skynet is finished with our modem. We don't barricade the door.
You can only catch the plague once, the saying goes. The washing line
is bowed by birds of prey, harpies and the Three Fates down one end.

We play Revelation bingo, but not Ragnarok quizzes, they end
in arguments. After our sixth Fourth Horseman, we don't want more.
The ice giants fight the killer robots to a draw. What's on the line
after the fallout and the earthquakes? Businesses still send
final notices for payment, they float on the rising flood up to my door,
and every bloody thing or nothing is an apocalyptic sign.

We've put a little food aside, water too. There is no sign
that home deliveries will re-start. If any television drama did not end
yet, it probably won't have time. Fenrir and Fenris scratch at the door,
asking to go for a walk. Sarah would take them, but she's more
tired today, wondering what it is all for. How should I send
her flowers? The roses brown and shrivel down their line.

Each tear should be death, each wrinkle and each line
an omen. Sweeping out the volcanic ash today, I see no sign.
Spraying for killer rodents and mutant cockroaches. Why send
doomsday at us, with alarum, sturm und drang? The end
shakes us every day, blink and we'd miss it. I can't do more.
When Sarah cries, the world ends, heaven latches its door.

We rehearse each line we're given. Each day the world ends
and nothing changes: each sign a new sign. We love as we can. No more
dooms that life can send us ravening through our open door.

Appraisal

He had an interesting turn of phrase, sometimes.
The kind of man it takes a long time to
work out whether he is joking or he is serious.
But he had a careful hand with a forklift
and knew his way around a Shipper's Letter of Instruction.
He could be a mean drunk, I've been told
but avoided the booze, and didn't bring problems to work.
He had been a meatpacker and a butcher's apprentice
when he was younger, and had learnt to stand all day
in the icy red numbness of the cold room,
peeling the seam of muscle with razor slices,
learning to hew the knot of dressed meat without
turning the wilful edge against the bone, and
steadying the anatomy of cold cuts with one steel glove.
He reckoned he was surgical in his day, with a sculptor's eye.
'Be careful', he'd tell us without expression,
'I know how to cut up a man and dispose of him'.
Then he'd laugh and clap us on the back,
but perhaps he took our measure with his hands.

Ice and Glass

You will be out of reach upon a wafer shelf of ice,
crabbing through dreams with bent knees, while
the ice snaps and smokes like a fragile simile.

But this has not happened yet. You sit with me, sketching
out your plans back in Queensland's provincial steamy pubs,
where glass is a verb to cold-eyed drunks sour with beer,

and ice grants visions. Veiny addicts become supermen,
fracturing their way through emergency wards, throwing
chairs through the looking glass, following Alice into the frost.

You once told me of the hapless kid who kicked in the church glass door
for the collection money, so that the priest had to save him
with his vestments: forever thinking of stained glass as arterial red.

In a pub near the Brisbane River viscid and luminous at dusk's edge
the water levels to a stretch of glass for the eight men who
slip their rowing boat through its cartesian warps.

We watch them lean back on the extraction, their arms
pendulum and piston, languid on the extensions, rapid
lunges, their reflection lagging out upon a sheer of glass.

I've seen you daydream through a store window at blue pup icebergs
and giant's fists hunkering in the flat bays of a travel agent's poster
as the Northern Lights flash green and turquoise above them.

But the auroras are spectral slivers and shards of a star's breath
and too cold for me. The sea's floating junk is a brittle wish
and all too chill. You will climb that mountain alone to the top.

The stars will be your cold witnesses, frigid and distant as
chipped nodules pressed into the galaxy's sore. Always icy
though each one is hotter than the first blood ever spilled.

The stars are too far away to be reached with apologies,
so we can describe them how we wish. The plummy
metaphor of glass: paste costume jewellery slung over space.

Similes for ice. Under the empty gaze of the shivering stars and
the shadow of the last peak swollen thick at the base, you think
of only one thing when you step out on each bare shelf of ice.

Sometimes it is warm enough for the sheeted ice to melt,
for the crevasse to give up the bodies it has chinked away,
but in this late freeze you walk across your mirror.

The mountain offers you a frozen scattering of light
that was water, a refraction eating away at this last hard climb.
A slick of glass. You skitter on the bound glissading wave.

It has not happened yet. It may never happen. These auguries
soap and fumble from the metaphor. A cold vision captured:
you step out under the heedless stars, the future slippery as glass.

Knot

Sorcerers and sovereigns of an age of wind:
makers of knots. They knew the truth of give
and take, the measure of strain, what could be held
by a thin rope, what could be bound in a slight loop.
Masters and their tools. Grown men come to blows over
the correct rigging, over the hawsers' twist and stay.
The art to be found in useful things: a crew could discern
by the stow of a coil whose hand wrangled.
Some knots were favourite children, others prodigal or cunning,
prone to turn on their makers, unravelling though trust was hung
by a thread, yet others in a roil of splices held to the bitter end.
My father is a maker of knots: last graduate and apprentice
of a lost class who can feel with their hands
the strange topology in a knot, the Mobius mathematics,
textures of plaits and twists, who can channel
the folded dimensions in a knot, the exotic spaces twined.
A skill not granted to his son. The things my father
can pull together, the weights he can carry
are beyond me, the casual sorcery in his fingers.
Like the arcane tangles of love, all I have learnt from him
is that the worth of a knot is in what it holds, and I have learnt
that even the strongest rope will break where it is tied.

On the Day You Launch

The future of the Earth is a series of goodbyes, so you
practise them in as many languages as you can. *Ciao, sayonara.*

How do you know what you should forgive, what you should regret,
what you will miss? *Auf wiedersehen, adieu*, to you and you and you.

This and this, and this, things you've learnt to hold,
tied to you with gentle strings, the umbilicus of memory.

Give it time, the attenuations of distance, the
ruthless shear of moments, accomplish any leave-taking.

What must the last days of the baiji dolphin have been like?
You've never heard of it, but now you find it's gone forever.

Pale and blind, lonely tag-end spirits of the Yangtze river, and a dam
flushed over them long before you were born, or could regret them.

Waiting in your hotel for take-off clearance, old documentaries blinking
at you in your room and the disoriented clicks of dolphins in your sleep.

Say goodbye to them and dress, the world has moved on, the rivers empty
and you are leaving. Life was always adept at forgetting the dead.

The future of the Earth is a one-way journey, a series of endings,
a solitary leap into space, loose cord unravelling behind you.

Anything you ever cared about must be forsaken one day, if only because
it cannot be held onto. You close your fingers, but it is gone.

You should begin now: cherish those things you must let go.
Cape Canaveral gives you a blue sky for your leaving. Say goodbye.

The rockets sweat in plumes of condensation and the gantries
sway and wave. Start with these: things are easiest to deny.

Long after the river had been given over to algal blooms, fishermen would
see those dolphins roll and dive. They could not abandon hope,

they could not abandon themselves, their childhood stories of solitary fins
slipping through water. To leave yourself is hardest, everything else can be survived.

Now the world's poor tug at the barbed wires of the launch site and wish to
join you. What wouldn't you part from here? Rising seas and stubble crops.

Today you can leap into the uncertain ocean of space and are privileged
to leave that old hegemony of Earth, the uncomfortable past.

How do we bear it? How do we let each second stream away
behind us, like the spent ejecta of a rocket pushed into the void?

Because we must. Because we were made for leave-taking and
for each severance, perhaps we are given something new, some brief gift.

I am saying goodbye too, did you know that? As you rehearse
detachment, I watch the sky for contrails spearing into blue haze.

I wonder at the ease of our partition: a lucky ballot and now seven languages
say goodbye to things worth forgetting. The last thing anyone forgives is the past.

Space is all departures and inertia: set a thing in motion and it moves
forever. This leaving pushes us away from each other and gravity does not hold.

Things fail. The night of the universe is a long outward breath
which does not repeat. You know that most of the universe is empty

so you have been saying goodbye, scrubbing out all that you can bear to leave.
Each heartbeat is an ending, not a beginning. You do not send me a message.

The other passengers tell you the trick is not to look back at the Earth fading.
Look forward, your spaceship dolphins outwards through the dark.

Afterword

These poems were written over the last decade, while the world changed around us and while we began to see that we are on an inevitable path toward environmental destruction and global warming. The world has become a meaner place over that time, a place of harsh politics, that values outrage over kindness, tribalism over empathy. It is not surprising that much of this context is embedded in these poems, like the backdrop of a play. There are poems about the end of the world in this collection, but few poems of hope. One of the main concerns in these poems is doubt and uncertainty. What can we truly know of the motivations of others? How can we be certain of love? Or that oldest of questions: is there such a thing as truth? These poems were written in the voices of many people, real and imagined, human and inhuman, sometimes even in the poet's own voice, although he is an unreliable narrator. Like the animals of the title, the poems are voices for human problems and troubles, for the little moments and cares of the human condition.

Notes

Animals With Human Voices

'Lady With an Ermine'. The 'Lady With an Ermine' is a Leonardo Da Vinci Painting of Cecilia Gallerani, the mistress of the Duke of Milan.

'What Happened to the Oysters'. Like many monocultures, Oysters are prone to sudden spikes in mortality. Some of these are due to viruses particular to them, some high mortality rates are attributed to the heavy metal content of the water they are in, or the presence of other pollutants or chemicals. This poem references some of the more well-known locations of these events.

'The Cold Snap'. The Phascogale is a tree-dwelling carnivorous marsupial which is known to attack and kill chickens. All other references to Stanthorpe locals or history are fictional.

'Laika Was a Dog'. In 1957, the stray dog, Laika, was the first animal to go into space. She died a week into her one-way journey, probably from overheating, but was able to prove that manned flights into space were possible. Later, her space-shuttle, Sputnik 2 burnt up upon re-entry into the Earth's atmosphere. There is now a statue in her honour in Russia, recognising the historical impact of her journey. "all the dogs of Europe barked" was taken from 'In Memory of W B Yeats' by W H Auden.

'Bezoar'. A bezoar is a stony accretion or ball of partially digested food found in a gut. It usually occurs due to illness or dietary issues. A gastrolith in contrast, is a stony object used by many animals and birds to help them digest food by breaking the food down.

Frozen men are often found in glacial environments preserved by rapidly freezing at the moment of death. Their bodies have been discovered with the evidence of their lives in remarkable conditions, including weapons and cloth and their last meal still identifiable in their stomachs.

Measures of Truth

'How Else But the Day' This poem is written in response to 'You, Andrew Marvel' by Archibald McLeish and follows the same format, number of stanzas and rhyme scheme. 'You, Andrew Marvel' had previously been written in response to 'To His Coy Mistress' by Andrew Marvel.

'Logical Fallacies of Alien'. A logical fallacy is reasoning which is incorrect and undermines the accuracy of the argument. There are many famous logical fallacies, some of which are listed in this poem. The fallacy may (or may not) be exemplified in the subsequent stanza.

This poem mainly refers to the *Alien* movie (1979, Director Ridley Scott) and its numerous sequels and prequels. 'Ripley', played by the actress Sigourney Weaver, is the lead in many of these movies. As a strong female lead, Ripley is often compared to Sarah Connor from the *Terminator* (1984, Director James Cameron) movie series, played by Linda Hamilton. 'Giger' in this poem, is a salute to HR Giger the artist who inspired the form of the 'aliens' and the overall mise en scene.

'The Cole Porter Effect'. The last line references a song by Cole Porter, the Big Band leader and song writer of the 1930s, 'Anything Goes'.

This poem refers to a number of true stories and legends including:

The entirely fictitious movie *The Legend of 1900* which describes the life of a piano prodigy who was born in 1900 and raised on an ocean liner, and who participated in a musical 'duel' with Jelly Roll Morton who had heard of his prowess. 1900's winning piece was so frenetic that a cigar was able to be lit from the red-hot piano strings after he finished playing. There really is an online forum that discusses whether or not this is possible.

Robert Johnson was a musician who lived from 1911 to 1938. The story goes that he happened to meet the devil on a deserted cross-roads in Louisiana and bartered his soul for the ability to be the greatest guitar player ever. The legend was reinforced by Robert Johnson himself who died young, and it is said his early death was due to the devil taking his part of the bargain.

Lucile is the name BB King gave to his guitar. The legend goes that BB King was caught in a fire that had been started at a club by two men fighting over a woman called Lucille. He was playing at the club and went back in to the flames to recover his guitar. BB King has named the guitar and every replacement 'Lucille' to remind himself never again to be so stupid as to run back into a fire.

How the Angels Covet Heaven

'**Dinners with Dead People**'. A common conversation starter is 'if you could have dinner with anyone who has ever lived, who would it be?' The people mentioned in this poem appear on the majority of lists. The details of each dinner attendant are based on real facts, or well-known stories: many people dispute that Elvis can appear in a list of dead people because he is not dead, but has instead been abducted by aliens. Another story has him killed by the Mafia. Einstein was a chain smoker who was known to wear his shoes without socks. Freud regularly consumed cocaine and favoured it as a means to improve concentration.

'**Cortege for Richard the Third**'. Richard the Third was King of England in the 15th Century. He died during the Battle of Bosworth Field. His body was not recovered, until 2012 when his remains were found in a city car park. Later DNA tests confirmed this discovery but also uncovered other unusual antecedents in his family tree. Shakespeare portrays him in The Tragedy of King Richard the Third as Machiavellian and disfigured by deformity. He was reinterred in Leicester Cathedral. In reality it is probable that his hunch was slight.

The Line Marker's Testimony

'**Fruit Picking**' responds to 'Digging' by Seamus Heaney. The 'Seamus' in this poem is intended to be the poet.

'**The Eighth Strike**'. The world record for being struck by lightning is seven strikes, held by Roy C Sullivan, but records are made to be broken.

'**The Superman Complex**' refers to George Reeves, the actor who played

Superman in the 1950s television series. At the age of 45, he died of a gunshot that was later ruled to be suicide. The poem also references two other actors, Adam West (who played Batman in the television series) and Johnny Weissmuller (who played Tarzan). Reportedly, George Reeves was always overshadowed by his role, and was never able to escape that typecasting once the series ended.

'**Knot**'. The making of a knot is as much art as skill and it is said that aficionados can recognise a knot made by someone they know. The bitter end, is the working part of the rope that is tied off.

Acknowledgements

I would like to thank the editors of the following journals where some of these poems first appeared:

Cordite, Island, the Newcastle Poetry Prize Anthology, Overland, Rabbit, Stilts, StylusLit, The Mozzie, Uneven Floor, Veronica Magazine and *Verity La.*

My thanks also to the judges and editors of the following competitions, where many of the poems in this collection won prizes or received commendation:

ACU Prize for Poetry 2017, 2018 and 2020, Bruce Dawe Poetry National Poetry Prize 2019, FAW John Shaw Neilson Poetry Award 2016, FAW Tasmania Poetry Prize 2015 and 2016, Glen Phillips Poetry Prize 2017, Gwen Harwood Poetry Prize 2018, Ipswich Poetry Feast—Open Category 2016, 2017 and 2018, Martha Richardson Memorial Poetry Prize 2016, Montreal International Poetry Prize 2020, the Moth Poetry Prize 2020, National Poetry Competition (United Kingdom) 2017, Newcastle Poetry Prize 2018 and 2020, Newcastle University International Poetry Competition 2020, Oxford Brookes International Poetry Prize 2017, Robyn Mathison Poetry Prize 2016, Tom Collins Poetry Prize 2019, The Plough Prize 2018, University of Canberra Vice Chancellor's Prize for Poetry 2018 and 2019, Val Vallis Award for an Unpublished Poem 2019, WB Yeats Poetry Prize 2018, Welsh International Poetry Competition 2019, Woorilla Poetry Prize 2019.

Special thanks to Ynes Sanz, Jenny Pollak, Roger Vickery, David Ades, and Margaret Clifford, whose advice on individual poems, inspiration and poetic community have been unstinting, honest and kind. All poets should have such poets as friends!

Finally, to all those Teachers who encouraged me to write and who only asked for a dedication on my first book in recompense. You know who you are.

About the Author

Damen O'Brien is an internationally award-winning poet, whose poems have won competitions in Australia, the United States, Wales, Ireland and England. Damen lives in Brisbane, Queensland and works for an Unmanned Aerial Vehicle company. Damen's poems have won the Moth Poetry Prize, the Peter Porter Poetry Prize and the Val Vallis Award for an Unpublished Poem amongst many others. He has been published in many of Australia's foremost literary journals including *Cordite, Southerly, Overland* and *Island*.

Printed in Australia
Ingram Content Group Australia Pty Ltd
AUHW020931050724
396636AU00002B/8